IN FOCUS...

SHARK LIFE

Camilla de la Bédoyère

Quarto Library

Quarto is the authority on a wide range of topics.
Quarto educates, entertains and enriches the lives of our readers—enthusiasts and lovers of hands-on living.
www.quartoknows.com

This library edition published in 2020
by Quarto Library,
an imprint of The Quarto Group.
26391 Crown Valley Parkway,
Suite 220
Mission Viejo, CA 92691, USA
T: +1 949 380 7510
F: +1 949 380 7575
www.QuartoKnows.com

Distributed in the United States and Canada by
Lerner Publisher Services
241 First Avenue North
Minneapolis, MN 55401 U.S.A.
www.lernerbooks.com

A CIP record for this book is available from the Library of Congress.

ISBN: 978 0 7112 5543 2

Manufactured in Guangdong, China CC042020

9 8 7 6 5 4 3 2 1

FSC www.fsc.org MIX Paper from responsible sources FSC® C008047

CONTENTS

Words in **bold** are explained in the Glossary on page 31.

THE SHARK

Sharks are the top **predator** in the ocean's food chain. All sharks are a type of fish, and they are found in oceans all over the world. They have been around since before dinosaurs existed.

The great white shark is an apex predator—it has no natural enemies.

A shark has a dorsal fin on its back to stop it from rolling to its side as it swims.

Fins

A shark has a large, triangular fin on its back that sticks up out of the water when it swims near the surface. This is known as the **dorsal fin**. A shark also has two large **pectoral fins**, one on each side of its body, behind its **gill slits**. A shark has other fins, too.

Breathing Underwater

Sharks use their **gills** to breathe in water. When they breathe, water enters their mouth. The water flows between their gills and out through the gill slits on the sides of their head. They absorb oxygen from the water as it passes through. Sharks have very wide jaws and some types, like this great white, have jagged, pointed teeth.

BITE-SIZE FACT

The biggest-ever great white shark was 23 feet (7 meters) long and weighed about 1,450 pounds (658 kilograms)!

SKELETONS AND SCALES

Most fish are bony fish. They have bony skeletons that give their bodies shape, power, and strength. Sharks, however, don't have hard bones. Instead, their skeletons are made from a bone-like material called **cartilage**, which is also strong, but it is lighter and less rigid than bone. In older sharks, the cartilage may have hardened and become more stiff and bone-like.

Colors and Patterns

Many sharks are dull colors, such as brown, gray, or black. These colors help them stay hidden in the deep, dark water. However, some sharks have interesting patterns. Colors and patterns can also help a shark stay hidden from view. This is called **camouflage**. A wobbegong shark's flat body, pattern of blotches, and frilled skin make it hard to spot on the seabed. Fish and **squid** that swim above mistake the shark for coral, rocks, or seaweed.

This swell shark has a spotted pattern to help it hide against the seabed.

Tough Skin

Shark skin is covered with scales that are coated with enamel—the same tough material that makes our teeth hard. These scales are called denticles. Denticles help water to move smoothly over a shark, so it can swim fast.

Scales from the skin of a spiny dogfish shark.

BITE-SIZE FACT

The rough surface of a shark's skin can tear the skin from a swimmer's leg.

Many sharks have a white belly. This helps them become invisible when seen from below against the light sky.

SWIMMING

Many types of shark must keep swimming, or they sink to the seabed. They also need to keep moving so that water pours through their gills and brings them the oxygen they need to breathe.

Some shark species prefer to swim in groups while hunting.

Different Strokes

Some **species**, such as the great white shark, push themselves through the water using the force of their powerful tail. Other sharks, for example the whale shark, thrust their bodies from side to side to propel themselves through the water. Their large fins help them balance. They swim much more slowly as they don't need to chase after their **prey**.

Shaped for Speed

The fastest sharks, such as the mackerel sharks, usually have a teardrop-shaped body and a crescent-shaped tail. This is similar to a fast-swimming tuna fish. Slower sharks, such as frilled sharks, are longer and more slender, and have longer tail fins.

BITE-SIZE FACT

Some sharks don't use their fins for swimming—they use them for crawling along the seabed instead!

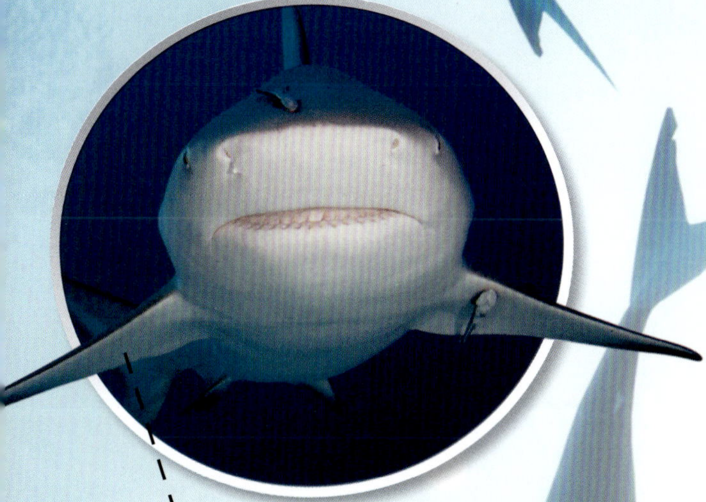

Large pectoral fins behind the gill slits help with balance.

At night, Port Jackson sharks stop swimming and sink to the seabed.

Changing Direction

Sharks cannot swim backward because their large pectoral fins are not able to bend upward like other fish. If a shark needs to move backward, it allows itself to be carried back by the water or it swims back around in a circle.

GIVING BIRTH

Most types of shark give birth to their young, which are called **pups**. A mother shark keeps her pups inside her body to protect them from predators while they grow. This time is called a pregnancy and it usually lasts from five to seven months. Spiny dogfish sharks, however, are pregnant for up to two years!

A newborn baby lemon shark and its mother.

Hammerhead sharks gather together in **shoals** at breeding time.

Nurseries

Mother sharks usually give birth in shallow water, such as coasts and bays. These birthing places are called nurseries. There is plenty of food for the pups to eat there, such as small fish, shellfish, and worms. The pups can also hide from predators among the rocks, sea grasses, and **algae**.

Port Jackson shark pups in their nursery.

BITE-SIZE FACT

Some shark pups eat one another while still inside their mother's body, until just one survives!

Growing Pups

Pups grow from eggs, which are inside the mother. While the pups grow, they get food from the egg yolk, or directly from their mother's body. The number of pups varies among species of shark. A sand tiger shark, for example, might have just one or two pups at a time, but blue sharks and whale sharks can give birth to more than 100 pups.

LAYING EGGS

Some sharks do not give birth to their young, but lay eggs outside their body, like other fish. One-third of all shark species lay eggs, which take about ten months to develop.

A shark embyro inside an egg case.

The dogfish shark's egg case anchors itself to rocks or seaweed to prevent it from floating away.

Protective Case

Each egg is protected from predators by a tough case, which is called a mermaid's purse. When the eggs hatch, the pups emerge. Most of them are about 8–12 inches (20–30 centimeters) long.

Keeping Safe

Most shark egg cases have long, curly strings that attach to coral or seaweed. This helps the egg to stay hidden among the foliage and to stop it from being carried away by the ocean's currents. Horn shark eggs do not have strings, so the mother twists them tightly into **crevices** using her mouth.

BITE-SIZE FACT

Fish often lay thousands of eggs at a time, but sharks lay far fewer. Horn sharks lay just two eggs at a time.

A lesser spotted dogfish shark hatching from an egg case.

Shark Pups

Baby sharks look like miniature adult sharks. They even have a full set of teeth. As soon as they hatch, they must take care of themselves, and many pups die before they can grow to adulthood.

GROWING UP

Sharks grow slowly and take many years to become full-sized adults. They then continue to grow throughout their lives.

BITE-SIZE FACT

The spiny dogfish is thought to live for up to 100 years. Whale sharks probably live even longer.

Swimming Off

As soon as shark pups are born, they swim away from their mother. It is important that they leave the parent quickly because some female sharks eat their own pups.

Sharks gradually grow larger as they get older.

Shark Hunters

Shark pups are preyed upon by other big fish, including sharks. Even some adult sharks are caught and eaten by other, larger sharks. However, most sharks are apex predators. This means they have no natural enemies —except people.

A silky shark pup.

This great white shark has a lot of scars and may be very old.

How Long Do Sharks Live?

Nobody is sure how long sharks live. Most of them probably live for fewer than 25 years, but a few types of shark have been known to live for much longer. Some of the larger species of female shark are not ready to breed until the female is between six and 18 years old. Most females produce young every two years.

WHAT DO SHARKS EAT?

Sharks are predators. This means that they hunt and eat other animals, from dolphins to little shrimp-like krill. They are the top predators in the ocean's food chain.

Fast sharks lunge at huge shoals of silvery fish, which are called bait balls.

This large shark is surrounded by smaller fish. Fish is a favorite food of most sharks.

Varied Diet

Although sharks eat a variety of foods, their diet is made up of mainly fish and **invertebrates**, such as squid and octopuses. Larger sharks catch bigger prey, including turtles, seals, and even dolphins. Some sharks eat animals that live on the seabed, such as crabs, starfish, sea urchins, and sea anemones.

Reef sharks in a feeding frenzy.

Feeding Frenzy

When sharks find their prey, they sometimes go into a feeding frenzy. This behavior happens when they find a group of injured or trapped fish, or another large source of food near the shore. The sharks become very excited and thrash around in the water, before moving in for the kill.

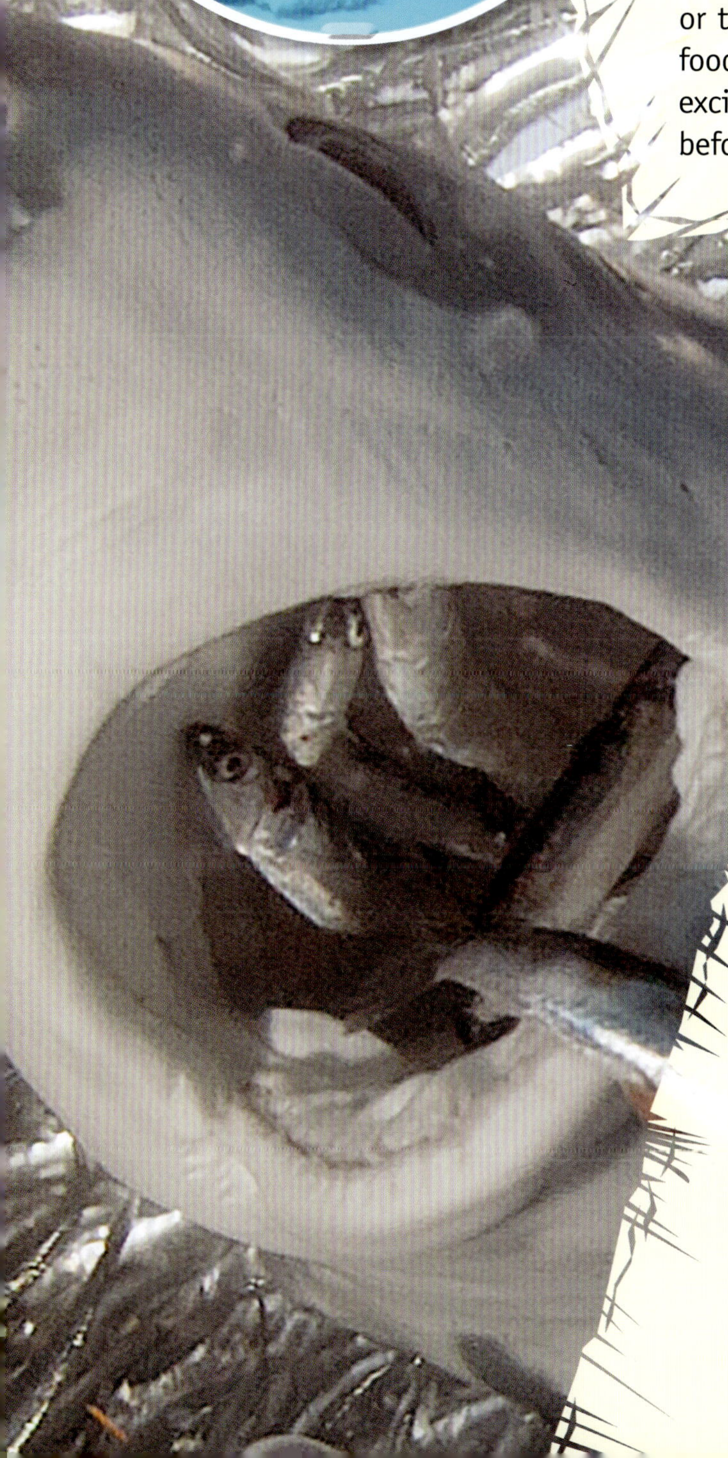

BITE-SIZE FACT

Some deep-sea sharks have chemicals in their skin, which they use to make light in order to attract prey.

How Much Do Sharks Eat?

Sharks are cold-blooded animals, which means they burn energy at a lower rate. This means that sharks do not have to eat as often as people think. Some sharks can have a huge meal and then not eat again for weeks.

PLANKTON EATERS

There are about 500 species of shark, but only three of them are plankton eaters. They feed on tiny ocean animals and plants, which are known as plankton. The way they eat is called filter feeding.

Each whale shark has its own unique pattern of spots on its skin.

A magnified view of plankton.

Food for Giants

Plankton includes baby fish, shrimp, and little animals called copepods. It also contains baby starfish, squid, and octopuses, which are smaller than a finger. Filter feeding sharks also eat small fish and jellyfish.

Friendly Fish

Whale sharks, megamouth sharks, and basking sharks are filter feeders. They are all large, slow-moving sharks and harmless to humans. Filter feeding sharks dive into deep water in the day, and swim to the surface at night to feed.

BITE-SIZE FACT

About 240,000 gallons (109,100 liters) of water pass through the enormous gills of the basking shark every hour when it is feeding.

Scoop and Suck

A filter-feeding shark feeds by swimming steadily forward with its huge mouth wide open, scooping up water and plankton as it goes. The seawater flows through its gills, where it is filtered. Then the shark eats the food that is trapped in the gills.

SCAVENGERS

A scavenger is an animal that eats dead animals or plants, or other food that might be considered garbage. Some animals that scavenge get most of their food this way, but all sharks that scavenge rely on hunting to get most of their food.

BITE-SIZE FACT

Sharks sometimes steal dead or dying fish from nets and fishing lines.

Tiger sharks mostly hunt living animals, but they are scavengers because their varied diet also includes dead animals.

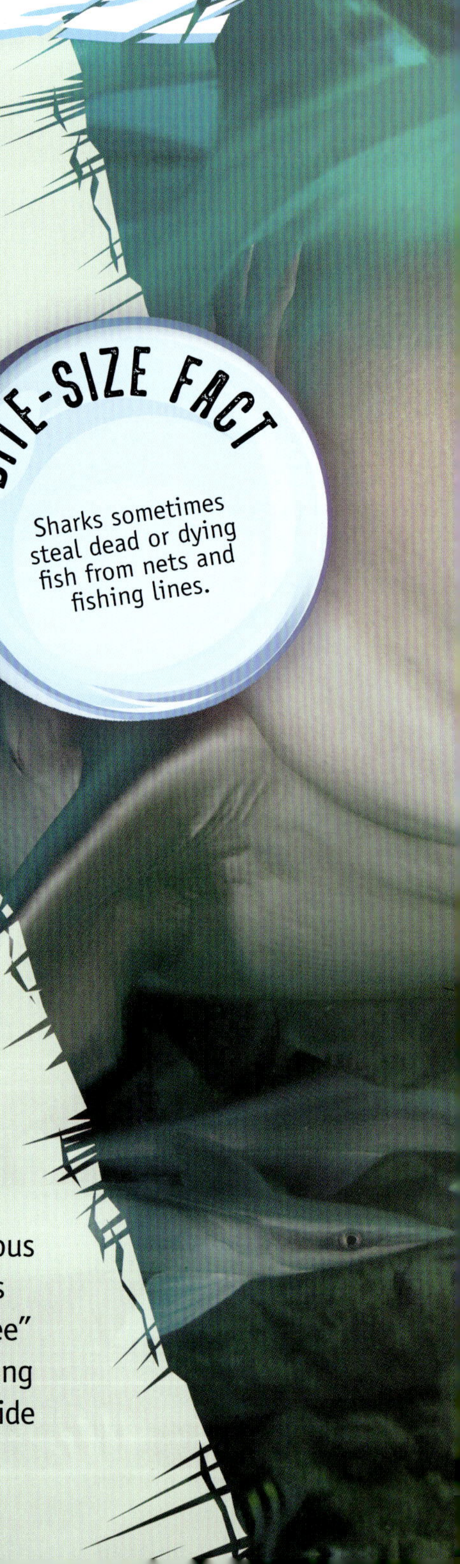

Free Meal

Hunting, chasing, catching, and killing an animal is dangerous for a predator, and uses a lot of energy. Eating a **carcass** is much easier, so it is no wonder that sharks may eat a "free" meal if they find one. If a scavenging shark eats something that gives it a stomachache, it can turn its stomach inside out and push the troubling thing out of its mouth.

A bull shark feeding on a carcass.

Unfussy Eaters

Tiger sharks, Mexican horn sharks, and Greenland sharks are well-known scavengers, but great white sharks also feast on a free meal when they can get it. Dead whales are a good source of protein and fat, so although great whites do not normally hunt whales, they will take bites out of a floating whale carcass if they find one.

This shark is eating a dead whale.

SHARK SENSES

Animals use their **senses** to get information about what is going on around them. Sharks have relatively large brains and seven main senses: sight, hearing, **electro-sense**, smell, taste, touch, and a pressure sense that allows them to detect movement.

Sharks have a super-sensitive sense of smell. They can sniff out one part of blood in one million parts of water.

Some sharks that live on the seafloor, like this carpet shark, have hanging tendrils, called barbels. They use these to touch and taste the seabed.

Smell and Taste

The senses of smell and taste are extremely important to sharks. They help a shark to find prey, but also to find mates. A shark's **nostrils** are on the underside of its **snout**, in front of its mouth. The taste buds are on the tongue.

Vision

Most sharks have good eyesight and can see near and far. Many species can also see color. Sharks that live in deeper water, like broadnose sevengill sharks, have large eyes to help them detect what little light there is. Most sharks do not have eyelids, but some have a special lower eyelid that protects the eyeball, especially during an attack.

A broadnose sevengill shark in deep water.

BITE-SIZE FACT

Some sharks may be able to track prey up to 1 mile (1.6 kilometers) away using their sense of smell.

Special Sense

Animals produce electricity in their muscles. Sharks can sense this using tiny, sensitive **pores** around their snout. They are called **ampullae of Lorenzini**. Sharks use this sense to find prey, including fish that are lying under a layer of sand on the seabed. Hammerhead sharks have a particularly strong electro-sense.

SENSING MOVEMENT

Sharks use changes in pressure to get detailed information about their surroundings. These changes in pressure help them hear, and find out if another animal is approaching.

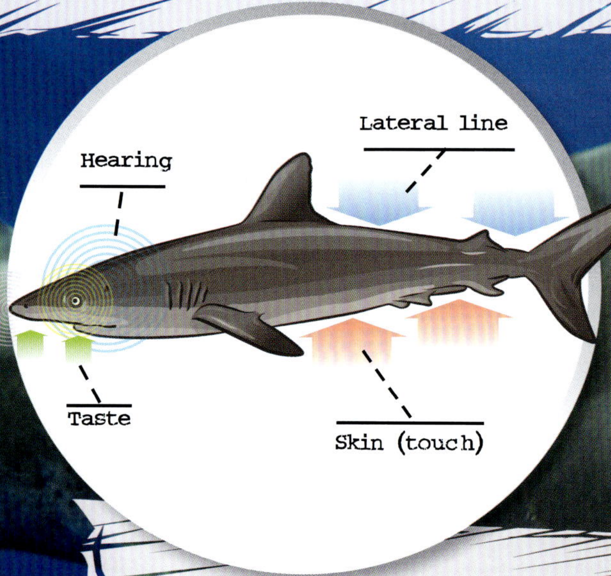

Movement

Sharks have a special sense organ called the **lateral line system.** It runs down each side of the body and around the head. It is lined with hairs that detect changes in pressure (vibrations) caused by water currents, and by other animals moving in the water.

Sounds

Sound is heard when vibrations affect the inner ears, which are inside the shark's head (sharks do not have outer ears). They are very sensitive to sound, especially low, deep sounds that can travel far in water. Sharks can figure out what direction sounds are coming from.

BITE-SIZE FACT

Injured animals give off stronger chemical and electrical signals than healthy animals.

Gray nurse shark

Working Together

Sharks use all of their senses to find out about the world around them. Their brains process all the information they receive from their sense organs to create a "picture" of other animals nearby. The predators can then decide what action to take.

SMART SHARKS

Scientists have discovered that sharks are intelligent fish, and that some sharks—such as the carpet, mackerel, and ground sharks—have brains that are as big and complex as some birds and **mammals**. Hammerheads are probably the most intelligent of all sharks.

At some tourist sites, sharks have learned that food will be put out for them every day. When they arrive to feed, divers are ready to photograph them.

Curious Fish

Many shark experts agree that great whites are curious sharks because they pop their heads out of water to see what is happening on the experts' boats. Great whites have also been seen to hunt and even play together.

Sharks in aquariums learn when it is feeding time.

BITE-SIZE FACT

Sharks may nudge and butt divers, because they have learned that divers sometimes give them food.

This whale shark is sucking on a fishing net from a boat

Learning to Behave

The most intelligent animals can learn from experience, change their behavior, and have good memories. Some sharks learn to follow fishing boats, so they can scavenge any dead fish thrown overboard. They have even been taught to travel through a maze to reach food in an **aquarium**. Some sharks have learned that they will be given food when a certain sound is made—and they can remember this signal many months later.

DISCOVERING SHARKS

Scientists observe sharks by diving with them, often inside safety cages. They also track sharks' behavior and movements with tagging.

A scientist interacts with a lemon shark.

BITE-SIZE FACT

A blue shark that was tagged near New York was found 16 months later some 3,600 miles (5,790 kilometers) away, off the coast of Brazil.

Tagging

An electronic device called a **tag** is attached to a shark's fin. The tag sends out signals that scientists use to follow the shark's journey, finding out how far it travels and where it goes.

Find Out More

There are many organizations that support sharks and work hard to make sure they survive. They have websites with more information on shark species, and they provide up-to-date news on the work scientists are doing to protect them.

This diver is swimming with a whale shark.

A diver can watch and film a great white shark from the safety of a cage.

Marine Parks

Many countries want to protect the oceans and the animals that live there, so they have set aside special areas where fishing boats cannot go. Sharks can live in these marine parks in safety, and tourists can visit them.

CREDITS

Key: FC = front cover, BC = back cover, t = top, b = bottom, c = center, r = right, l = left.

Alamy:
20-21 Michael Patrick O'Neill.

Dreamstime:
12bl Jilliansuzanne, 12-13 Marleenwolters; 21br Mark Higgins;

FLPA:
1 Reinhard Dirscherl; 9br Fred Bavendam/Minden Pictures; 10bl Norbert Probst/Imagebroker; 13br Jean-Michel Mille/Biosphoto; 14-15 Imagebroker, 15tr Pete Oxford/Minden Pictures, 15br William J. Howes; 16bl F1online/F1online; 17tl Norbert Wu/Minden Picture; 18-19 Reinhard Dirscherl, 19cr Colin Munro; 22cl Colin Marshall, 22-23 Norbert Wu/Minden Pictures; 24-25 Norbert Wu/Minden Pictures, 25bl Norbert Wu/Minden Pictures; 27cr Mike Veitch/ Biosphoto; 28-29 F1online/F1online;

Getty:
18bl Andy Mann.

Nature Picture Library:
16-17 Chris & Monique Fallows

Science Photo Library:
7tl EYE OF SCIENCE.

SeaPics.com:
10-11 Doug Perrine, 11tr Andy Murch.

Shutterstock:
FC OutdoorWorks; BC wildestanimal; 2 Dray van Beeck; 4br jamen percy, 4-5 Derek Heasley, 5tl Elsa Hoffmann, 5br Dray van Beeck; 6br NatalieJean, 6-7 Greg Amptman; 8-9 Digital Storm, 9cl Shane Gross; 20cl A Cotton Photo; 23tl Fiona Ayerst; 24cl LSkywalker; 26cr A Cotton Photo, 26-27 tororo reaction; 28bl Greg Amptman, 29tr Krzysztof Odziomek; 30 A Cotton Photo.

The publisher gratefully acknowledges the permission granted to reproduce the copyright material in this book. Every effort has been made to trace copyright holders and to obtain their permission for the use of copyright material. The publisher apologizes for any errors or omissions in the above list and would be grateful if notified of any corrections that should be incorporated in future reprints or editions of this book.

GLOSSARY

algae
simple plants and plant-like living things usually found in the sea. Seaweed is a type of algae

ampullae of Lorenzini
small sensors on a shark's head that detect electrical signals made by another animal's body

aquarium
a large glass tank, filled with water, where fish and other ocean animals can live

camouflage
an animal's coloring that helps it to blend into the background

carcass
the body of a dead animal

cartilage
a type of bone-like material that is strong but bendier than bone

crevice
a crack in the sea bed or rocks

dorsal fin
the fin on a shark's back

electro-sense
a sense that allows sharks to detect the electricity made in other animals' bodies

gill slits
the openings on a shark's body that lead to the gills

gills
the parts of a fish's body where oxygen is removed from the water so the fish can breathe

invertebrate
an animal that does not have bones or a skeleton

lateral line system
a system of sense organs that allows a fish to feel movement and vibration in the water

mammal
an animal that has hair or fur, gives birth to its young, and feeds them with milk

nostril
the hole that leads into a snout or nose

pectoral fins
the fins on the side of a fish's body, behind its head

pore
a small hole in the skin

predator
an animal that hunts and kills other animals to eat

prey
animals that are hunted by predators

pup
baby shark

sense
the ability to notice changes in the environment

shoal
a group of fish

snout
the mouth and nose of a shark

species
a type of animal or plant. Animals from the same species mate with each other and have young

squid
a soft-bodied ocean animal with eight arms and two tentacles

tag
a small device that is attached to an animal so its movements can be tracked

INDEX